Warum gerade ich?

D1673348

Warum muss ausgerechnet mir sowas passieren?

„Mach was vernünftiges, was solides!" hat meine Mutter immer gesagt. Irgendwann also wollte ich Möbelkatalog werden – da hatte ich noch Ziele! Chrom und Edelstahl, Mahagoni und Samt wollte ich zeigen; ich wollte Hochglanz und Sonderfarben, Lack und richtig gutes, gestrichenes Papier. Die ganz großen internationalen Namen – ich sage nur: Italien, Schweiz …

Doch dann kam der Moormann.

Der *Moormann*, das muss man sich mal vorstellen! Ein Schreiner aus Bayern! Nur so zur Verdeutlichung: der Mann macht *Klapptische* und *Regale, die wackeln*! Und das Schlimmste ist: die quatschen mich hier alle voll! Bin ich jetzt der Psychiater oder was? Was geht mich eine Leiter mit Höhenangst an? Ich kann nicht mehr, ich bin am Ende, aus, vorbei, jetzt bin ich reif für die Couch …
Ich wünschte wirklich, Sie würden mich einfach wieder zurücklegen und nicht weiter aufschlagen. Kommen Sie schon, *bitte*! Legen Sie mich einfach zurück auf den Stapel oder gleich ins Altpapier. Das ist doch kein großer Wunsch …

Learn a proper trade, that's what my mother always said.

Somewhere along the line I wanted to be a furniture catalogue – those were the days, when I still had plans! Chrome and stainless steel, mahogany and velvet, that's what I wanted, trying to show off I suppose; I wanted glossy colours and special finishes, varnishes and really nice handmade paper. And all the big international names. Italy, Switzerland, to name a few.

And along came Moormann!

Moormann, put yourself in my position. A carpenter from deepest, darkest Bavaria! Let me spell it out: He makes **folding tables** and **shelves that wobble**! And the worst thing is, they all chew my ear off the whole day long! Do they think I'm their own personal psychiatrist? What do I care if a ladder is afraid of heights. I can't take it any more. This is the end. Finito. Over and done with. Show me where the couch is.

I really hoped they would put me back where they found me, never to flip through my pages again. Leave me alone **please**. Just put me back on the pile or toss me into the recycling bin. Not much to ask for is it?

Waren Sie schon mal in New York? Vielleicht auf dem Empire State?

So komme ich mir jeden Morgen vor.

Ich schlage die Augen auf und denke nur:

„bloß nicht nach unten sehen, bloß nicht nach unten sehen …"

– und trotzdem: mein Blick fällt nach unten

und schon wird mir übel,

das Herz rast und ich habe ganz wackelige Knie …

In meinem Beruf ist Höhenangst natürlich fatal!

… ich meine, wer würde sich mir noch anvertrauen,

wenn er von meiner Höhenangst wüsste?

Sicher, ich übe jeden Tag und ich glaube, es ist auch schon besser geworden.

Ich brauche einfach jemanden, an den ich mich mal anlehnen kann,

einen verlässlichen Partner an meiner Seite,

verstehen Sie?

6　7
8
1/23　2
3
5　9　10
4　11
3　4
1
2
8
7
5
6
12
11
10　9
15　16
14　13
20　21
19 18　17
25　26 27
21/35　22 24 23
20　19 34　22
30　33
29　31 32
28
16
15
18　17
14　12
13

HochAcht ist von großer Stabilität und doch anlehnungsbedürftig. Obwohl sie einer Leiter gleicht, ist sie vielmehr ein Sitz-Objekt und somit nicht für den alltäglichen Gebrauch als Leiter vorgesehen. Die zweite Stufe ist zum Sitz, die dritte zur Lehne ausgebildet. Die oberste Stufe ist nach hinten verlängert und bietet so eine Lehnfläche wie auch eine Ablagemöglichkeit. Buche massiv.

'HochAcht' is highly stable but still needs to lean up against something. Despite looking like a ladder, it is more an object to sit on than a common ladder to be climbed. The second step is a seat, and the third offers a chance to lean back. The highest step acts as an extension, creating a leaning device as well as a filing possibility. Solid beech.

HochAcht   Cecilie Manz   2000   h/h 238   b/w 51,4   t/d ca. 90

Haben Sie schon mal etwas von der Entdeckung der Langsamkeit gehört? Ich habe c
eine ganz eigene Definition bilden können. **Mein Name ist Programm**. Ich liebe d:
Spontanität, die Geschwindigkeit, schnelles Anpassen an neue Situationen – und dan.
muss der Moormann ausgerechnet in Bern einen Laden aufmachen! Ja, glaubt de
denn, dass ich mich in diesem Land entfalten kann? *(Schwyzerdütsch nachahmend)* n u r n ü
h u u u d l e . Nun kommt zu meinem neuen Wohnort auch noch eine massive Ver
sagensangst hinzu. Aber meinem Bruder in Wien geht es da ganz ähnlich ...

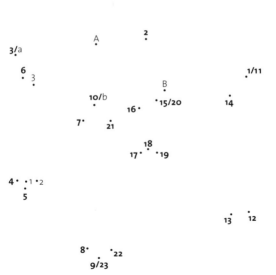

Er lässt sich mit einem Handgriff ausein-
anderfalten, ist aber trotz seines geringen
Gewichtes stabil und standfest. Für die
platzsparende Aufbewahrung des zusam-
mengeklappten Tisches wird eine Wand-
halterung mitgeliefert. Zudem erlaubt
die durchdachte Kantenausbildung eine
fugenlose Reihung mehrerer Tische.
FU (Sperrholz, Birke), natur klarlackiert,
weiß und Linoleum schwarz.

*It only takes a moment to unfold, yet is
sturdy and stable despite its light weight.
A wall hook is provided as a space-saving
storage feature for the table when folded
up. The ingenious shape of the table edges
makes it easy to combine with other tables
in series. FU (birch plywood). Natural clear
varnish, white, linoleum black.*

Last Minute Hauke Murken 1992 h/*h* 74 b/*w* 81 t/*d* 76

Lassen Sie sich von meinem
schlichten Äußeren nicht täuschen!
Ich bin sicher, dass in mir etwas
ganz Großes steckt.

Sie sind ein zu beneidender
Mensch, dass Sie meine Bekannt-
schaft machen dürfen.

Setzen Sie sich und genießen Sie
einfach diesen grandiosen Augen-
blick.

Glauben Sie mir, mit uns beiden,
das kann nur ein Siegerteam sein.

Stellen Sie sich nur die Schlagzeilen
vor. Ich bin sicher: *das* wird durch
die internationale Presse gehen ...

4•   5••7   8••11   •12

27/1   2   3
            • 19/A   6
                      9••10   13••14/B

26• •23   •20/a   •15/b

22• •19
25• •18 •18
•24   •15   1
21• 28 •17/21   16• •2/29
17• •20 14• 10• •4   3
•16   11   7

13•
•12

9• 5
•8   6

Das Banksystem lässt sich individuell zusammenstellen. In die Trägerschiene werden Beine eingeschraubt und verschiedene Sitzelemente in beliebiger Reihenfolge und Ausrichtung fixiert. Die Utensilienbox bietet Stauraum. Die Trägerschiene ist in zwei Längen erhältlich, maximal können entweder 3 oder 5 Sitze montiert werden. Trägerschiene FU (Sperrholz, Birke) klarlackiert. Beine Ahorn massiv, klarlackiert. Sitze FU (Sperrholz, Birke) Ahornfurnier, klarlackiert.

This bench system can be assembled to meet your needs. The legs screw into the base rail, with the various seating elements sliding into place in any order and direction. The integrated box provides storage space. A maximum of either three or five seats can be attached to a base rail that comes in two different lengths. Base rail FU (birch plywood), clear varnish. Legs solid maple, clear varnish. Seats FU (birch plywood), maple veneer, clear varnish.

Deutsche Bank Bisjak, Graf und Richter 1998 h/h 45/90 t/d 43 l 129/215

Ich bin eine Insel, ich bin eine Insel, ich bin eine Insel ...

ich bin eine Insel, ich bin eine Insel,
ich bin eine Insel ...

ich bin eine Insel,
ich bin eine Insel, ich bin eine Insel ...

(liest hmm ... Miller, Hesse, Freud – Freud???...)
Ich bin eine Insel, ich bin eine Insel, ich bin eine Insel ...

3

• **2/**1

• **11**

12

19 •

4

2
• **20**

...eine Insel...

14
• **1/9**
10/33

13/17 •
• h
18/24 •
• **15**
32 • • **8**

23
21/27 • **22**
28 •
25 • • **16/e**
31 •
• **6**
• g

A •
• **26/**a
d/f
a

4 •
29 •
• b
a

• c

5 •
30/B •
b
• **5**

3
b

• **6/C**

,Hieronymus im Gehäuse', ein Strandkorb am Meer, ein Bahnabteil – Lese+Lebe ist ein Raum im Raum, der zum Entspannen und zum Schmökern im Lieblingsbuch einlädt. Die Rückseite bildet ein Regal. Wahlweise links oder rechts kann die Rückenlehne als Tisch heruntergeklappt werden. Unter der Sitzfläche verborgen gibt es ausziehbare Fußstützen und Schubkästen mit viel Stauraum. FU (Sperrholz, Birke) schwarz oder weiss. Kissen: Leinengewebe in den Farben rot oder orange. Teppich: Ziegenhaar und Schurwolle, rot oder orange, schwarz gekedert.

A beach chair by the sea, a dining compartment on a train – 'Lese+Lebe' is a room in a room, one which invites you to just sit down, relax and browse your favourite book. The standing back comprises the shelves. The backrest can be folded down to the left or the right to make a table. Hidden under the seat are extendible footrests and drawers with lots of space. FU (birch plywood), black or white. Pillows, linen, red or orange. Carpet, goat hair and wool, red or orange, black edging.

Lese+Lebe Nils Holger Moormann 2004   h/*h* 140 b/*w* 122 t/*d* 72
Teppich/*carpet* l 200/375 b/*w* 200

Nein, Nein, Nein!!

      ...   ...

das Buch hat keine Poesie ... der Autor ist vollkommen überschätzt ...

      ... – – – ...

          vielleicht darf ich auch mal

... vollkommen ...

      ... also der Autor ...

... hat es Erotik? Ich glaube nicht.

      ...dennoch –

Es langweilt mich ...

         also das ist mir jetzt zu pauschal.

      ...   ...

... ich lese keine Manuskripte, GRUNDSÄTZLICH *nicht!!*

    (*fängt langsam an, sich zu drehen ...*)

c

d•   •b
13• 14/18   **C**   **2**
       17•   **6**   **•3/7**
            a/e

D•   •**B**
   15/22 16   •f   **•5**
          21• c   **•4/11**
              A/E **•10**

d•   •b
   19/26 **•20** **•F**
          C   **•9**
   25•   a/e   **•8/15**
              •14
              f

D•   •**B**
       •24   **•13**
   23•   **•6**   **•12**
       A/E **•18**
     29•

F
7/11•   **1**   •1/5
   12•   **•17**
10•   •28 **•16**   •2
   •27
        4/8

3/9

Buchstabler verstaut mit minimalem Materialaufwand ein Maximum an Büchern. Das Regal wird gesteckt, ist drehbar, steht frei im Raum und kann nach Bedarf Etage für Etage in die Höhe wachsen. Voll bestückt wird Buchstabler nahezu unsichtbar und überlässt die Bühne den Büchern, die mit sichtbarer Frontpage präsentiert werden. Regalseiten und Tablare FU (Sperrholz, Birke) schwarz oder weiß. Buchfixierung Federstahl. Sockel Zementguss weiß-grau. Spannseil Synthetikfaser.

Using a minimum amount of material, 'Buchstabler' stores a maximum amount of books. The rack is fastened together, can be rotated, stands freely and, if necessary, can be built higher and higher. When full, the unit can hardly be seen, leaving the spotlight on the books, displayed with their covers visible. Side panels and shelf boards FU (birch plywood), black or white. Bookends, spring steel. Base, cement-cast, white-grey. Tensioning cable, synthetic fibre.

Buchstabler Tom Fischer 2004 h/*h* variabel/*variable*

Fächer lichte Höhe/*compartment height* 23 b/w 33 t/*d* 33

Mein ████████████████████ egal! ████████████████████████████████████ auf!

Das ist ████████████████ Aber das begreift ja keine ████████ !

hoch, runter, rein, raus, ihr ██

██

██

██

██

Macht doch, was ihr wollt!

VE
a/e
B
b

1/25 4 5   8 9   12 13   16 17   20 21 24

2   3 6   7 10   11 14   15 18   19 22 23

24 21 20   17 16   13 12   9 8   5 4   1/25

23 22 19   18 15   14 11 10 7   6 3   2

1/25   4 5   8 9   12 13   16 17   20 21   24

2   3 6   7 10   11 14   15 18   19 22   23

20   17 16   13 12   9 8   5 4   1/21

19   18 15   14 11   10 7   6 3   2

1/33 4 5   8 9 12 13   16 17 20 21   24 25   28 29 32

2   3 6   7 10 11 14   15 18 19 22   23 26   27 30 31

20   17 16   13 12   9 8   5 4   1/21

19   18 15   14 11   10 7   6 3   2

1/29 4 5   8 9   12 13   16 17   20 21   24 25   28

2   3 6   7 10   11 14 15 18   19 22   23 26 27 c

C

Egal ist in der Höhe sowie in der Fachein-
teilung variabel. Die in vier verschiedenen
Höhen erhältlichen Fächer können auch
nach dem Aufbau in der Breite verändert
werden. Schiebetüren und Schubkästen
ergänzen das System, das ohne Werkzeug
montiert wird. MDF natur, weiß, grau,
schwarz oder FU (Sperrholz, Birke) weiß,
schwarz. Schiebetüren: Acrylglas glas-
look satiniert, rot, orange, blau, grün.
Schubkästen zusätzlich in MDF pastellblau, pastellgrün, orange, rot.

*'Egal' is a shelving system comprising com-
partments with variable heights and
widths. With their four different heights,
the width of the compartments can be
rearranged after assembly as desired. The
system offers shifting compartments and
sliding doors. It can be assembled without
any tools. Either MDF natural, white, grey,
black or FU (birch plywood) white or black.
Sliding doors, plexiglass, glass-look satin,
red, orange, blue, green. Drawers addition-
ally available in MDF, light blue, light green,
orange, red.*

Egal Axel Kufus   2001   h/h 10,7/16,8/22,9/35,0 b/w 116,8/174,4/232,0/289,6 t/d 36,5

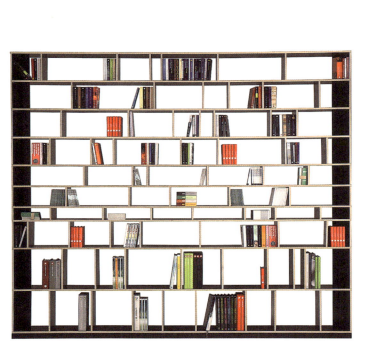

Mist, c'est chaque nuit la mème rêve...
es ist immer dassälbe, dersälbe immer wiedèrkehrende Trâum...

Oui, immèr. Je tombe ...
isch falle und falle immer tiefèr und tiefèr ...

                            ... auf ein kleine niedlische 'und!
immer wieder und wieder.

Non, bis jetzt war morgens immer alles in Ordnung.

8

6•

9• •1/5
10

7/g•

c• 2/f •14

b/d• e•   8

4/a   9/13   •D

12/**C**

3/**A**   **B**

15/**d** **7** •**6/**22

10/**c** •16

17/21
a   c

11/**b**   •b/d

5/23/g
4

•20/a

•18/f   •**3**

•e

24
19/25• **1**

2

Das horizontal oder vertikal an der Wand angebrachte Stahlblech bildet die Basis für eine Vielzahl von Möglichkeiten: Boxen mit magnetischer Rückseite haften daran in jeder gewünschten Position. Je nach Anzahl, Größe und Anordnung der Boxen entsteht immer wieder ein völlig neues Regal. Boxen FU (Sperrholz, Birke) natur klarlackiert, weiß, schwarz. Wandblech Stahlblech, warmgewalzt, gezundert.

A metal sheet mounted horizontally or vertically on the wall provides an endless variety of possibilities: boxes with magnetic backs stick to it in any position. Depending on the number and size of the boxes, a new shelf is available with each new arrangement. Boxes FU (birch plywood) natural clear varnish, black, white. Wall attachment, sheet steel, plated, wax treated.

Magnetique Swen Krause 2000 Boxen/*boxes* h/*h* 30/16/26 b/*w* 30/60/45 t/*d* 21/15,5/18
Wandblech/*wall attachment* h/*h* 192 b/*w* 28 t/*d* 1,9

Wissen Sie, eigentlich sieht man mir meine Klangfülle nicht gleich an...
... aber es spielt ja eh' keiner mit mir.

Ja so ein Blödsinn, natürlich kann man auch auf einer Saite
alles spielen, der Klang kommt natürlich vom Körper ...

Haben Sie schon mal ein Menuett mit Handtüchern und halbvollem
Shampoo gespielt? Versuchen Sie mal! Na los ...

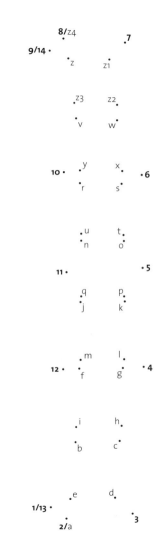

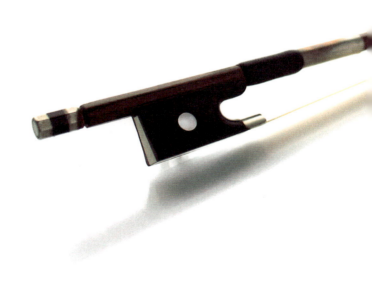

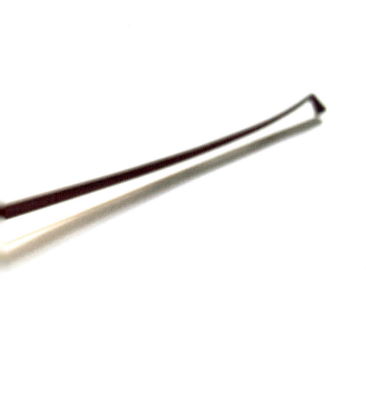

Das Gespannte Regal ist längst ein Design-Klassiker. Sein charakteristisches Stahl-seil ist keineswegs nur Dekoration, sondern sorgt für Spannung und Stabilität. Das Regal besteht aus gewachstem, warm-gewalzten Stahlblech (3mm) und ist geschweißt.

'Gespanntes Regal' has long been con-sidered a classic by the world of design. Its characteristic steel cable is by no means decoration, but provides the tension and stability it needs to remain upright. Waxed, plated 3mm sheet steel, welded.

Gespanntes Regal   Wolfgang Laubesheimer   1984   h/*h* 240   b/*w* 39,2   t/*d* 31

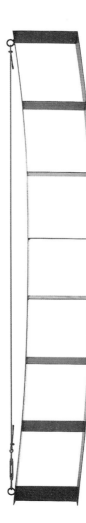

Mein lieber Herr,
in Ihrer Praxis
das Chaos herrscht ganz fürchterlich.
Sie meinen, ich sei nur ein Möbel –
ich denke aber, also bin ich …

Wenn Blicke in die Ferne schweifen,
Gedanken noch verschwommen sind,
beginnt in mir heranzureifen
in langen Zügen Dichters Kind.

Und schon die Zeilen griffbereit
um Handesbreiten vor mir liegen.
In den Gedanken geh' ich weit,
denn die Gedanken sollen siegen …

Mir steht der Sinn nach Rationalem,
Erkenntnis klar in reiner Form,
das Ding an sich erliegt Banalem!
Der Weltenordnung Postulat: die Norm.

Bedeutung ist's, wonach ich strebe;
mir steht Sinn nach Unsterblichkeit.
Verstand bedeutet lese, lebe –
besinne Dich zu jeder Zeit.

Vernunft, Vernunft hör' ich mich sagen,
und glaubt mir, ich erkenn' es wohl:
Die Transzendez besteht aus Fragen,
die Transzendenz ist innen hohl.

(… geht raus …)

Da geht er hin und kann nicht fassen,
die Urgewalt schaut hinterher –
wir können es von mir aus lassen,
dann bleibt die Transzendenz halt leer.

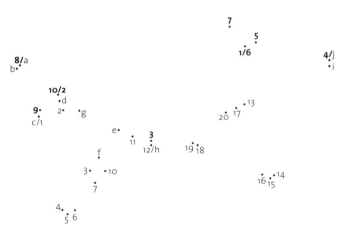

n'est

pas

Kant sorgt für Ordnung auf dem Schreib-
tisch. In der eingeknickten Arbeitsplatte
werden Bücher, Ordner und tausend an-
dere Dinge, die das Leben auf dem Schreib-
tisch durcheinanderbringen, übersichtlich
verstaut. Tischplatte Birkensperrholz
weiß laminiert oder Oberfläche Linoleum
schwarz, blau oder rot. Beine: Ahorn massiv.
Mini Kant, Mini Kant Bücherfreund,
Kant Sekretär: Tischplatte FU (Sperrholz
Birke) schwarz oder weiß.

*'Kant' brings organisation to the writing
desk. The surface dips down at the rear,
and offers a place to stow books, files and
thousands of other things that threaten
to overwhelm us. Table top, birch plywood
laminate, white or with surface in linoleum
black, blue or red. Legs, solid maple.
Mini Kant, Mini Kant Bücherfreund, Kant
Sekretär, table top FU (birch plywood),
black or white.*

Kant Patrick Frey, Markus Boge 2002

Mini Kant h/*h* 45 b/*w* 43 t/*d* 53
Mini Kant Bücherfreund
h/*h* 45 b/*w* 130 t/*d* 53

Kant Sekretär h/*h* 74 b/*w* 120/140 t/*d* 85,5
Kant Sitztisch h/*h* 74 b/*w* 160/190 t/*d* 105
Kant Stehtisch h/*h* 111 b/*w* 160/190 t/*d* 105

Wen darf ich melden? Sie haben doch einen *Termin?*

Oh ich **bedaure** zutiefst. *Ohne* kann ich Sie **nicht** anmelden.

Sie müssen jetzt nicht pampig werden, da könnte ja *jeder* kommen.
... raus jetzt und nehmen Sie Ihren Hut und Ihren Mantel wieder,
ich bin schließlich nicht **Ihre** Garderobe!

3 •2

25 26
24 •27
g f c b
5 4 28/A
6
1/23 •B

21
•20

17 •16

30 31
29/3 •32
33/2

22/4
19/1

13 12
14/34 11
a 10
18 e d
h
15 •9
7 8

Eine ineinanderschiebbare Rohrkon-
struktion ermöglicht die Anpassung der
Garderobe an unterschiedliche Raum-
situationen. Ihre Breite ist vor der Montage
stufenlos von 85 bis 150 cm zu variieren.
Durch ein mitgeliefertes Kupplungsstück
lassen sich beliebig viele Garderoben
zu einem System erweitern. Aluminium
eloxiert, Gurte Gewebegummi.

*A nesting tube construction lets this coat
rack adapt to a variety of situations.
Prior to installation, the width can be
adjusted anywhere between 85 cm and
150 cm. A coupling element allows several
racks to be combined into a single system.
Elastic belts made of textile tape serve as
the hat rack. Aluminium anodised.*

Expander Benjamin Thut   1992   h/*h* 35   b/*w* 85–150   t/*d* 30

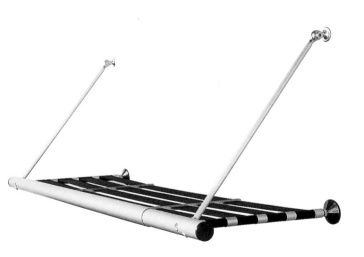

Tohaŋtu kiŋ c'eyaš Haŋhepi Wi kiŋ he Aŋpetu Wi kiŋ inuŋpa kte haŋtaŋš micaŋte kiŋ mni okášpe kiŋ el kiciħa po.

Wašicu Wakaŋ kiŋ he wiokipi šni uŋ waapiya okihi hwo?

(Sprache der Lakota-Indianer. Sinngemäß:
Wenn der Mond die Sonne zum zweiten Mal besiegt hat,
dann begrabt mein Herz an der Biegung des Flusses.
Hat der weiße Mann, der durch die Couch spricht, eigentlich
auch ein Mittel gegen Heimweh?)

9 •11
7 •
6 • • 10
14
• •15

8
•

12
5 • •13
•16
4 • •1/6
1/32 •• 2 5
•
b
•

•3 17
•a/d 2 •

c
•
4
•
31• •3
•20
30• •23
•24

•
27

29• •28   22• •21

26• •25

Hut ab bietet eine Vielzahl von Hänge-
möglichkeiten. Die Ausformungen an
den Stangenenden sind sowohl für Bügel
als auch für Kleideraufhänger geeignet.
In der Beuge zwischen langen und kurzen
Holmen finden Taschen Halt. Die Gelenke
zwischen den Holmen bieten durch ihre
Hakenform weitere Optionen. Hut ab lässt
sich mühelos zusammenklappen und
platzsparend verstauen. Esche unbehandelt oder Nussbaum geölt, die Haken
bestehen aus eloxiertem Aluminium.

*'Hut ab' (Hats Off) can be suspended in a
number of ways. The shape of the pole
ends makes them ideal for hanging both
hangers and clothes hooks. There is room
for bags in the bend between the short
and long rods. The joints between the rods
serve various purposes due to their hooked
shapes. The item is easily folded together
and stored in a minimum of space. Rods,
solid ash or oiled walnut. Hooks, anodised
aluminium.*

Hut ab   Konstantin Grcic   1998   h/*h* 184   b/*w* 63   t/*d* 63

Kan ic mic be Ihne anlehne ?

Verlassensängst ? N Si sin gu
Habe Si kein Angs vor Alleinesei ?

Ic brauch eine starke Partne .
Allein bi ic nicht .

Ic mu mic einfac anlehne könne .

Wan da angefange ha ?

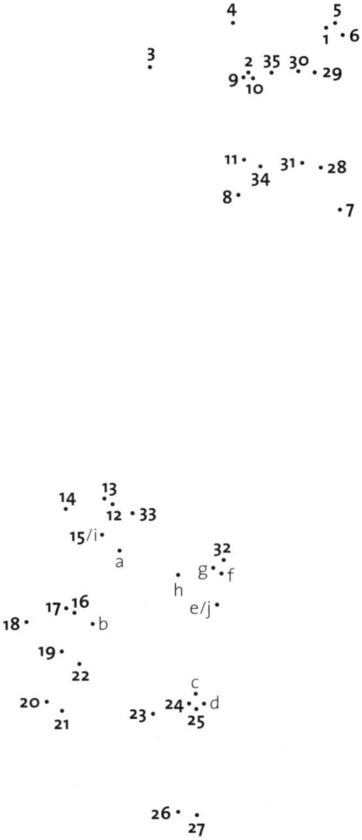

4

5

3

1 • 6

2 35 3O 29

9

10

11 • 31 • 28

34

8 •

• 7

14 13

12 • 33

15/i•

a

32

g • • f

h

e/j •

17 • 16

18 • • b

19 •

22

c

24 • • d

20 • 23 • 25

21

26 • •

27

Eine leichte und handliche Bibliotheksleiter, die an nahezu jedes Bücherregal angelehnt werden kann. Die Ablage lädt zum Nachschlagen oder Notieren vor Ort ein und verleiht der Leiter den Charakter eines Stehpultes. Die beiden Holme aus massiver Buche sowie die Stufen und die Ablage aus Formholz sind geölt. Die Anlehnfläche ist mit grauem Filz beschichtet.

Light-weight and easy-to-use library steps that can be leaned against virtually any bookcase. The book-rest invites you to stop and peruse a volume or can be used as a writing surface, turning a ladder into a lectern. Side elements, solid beech, oiled. Steps and book rest, moulded plywood, oiled. Angled surface and shelving covered in grey felt.

Step Konstantin Grcic 1995 h/*h* 150 b/*w* 51 t/*d* 50

Warum eischendlich sieht mer, dass isch von drübn bin?
steht das mir nu auf der Stirne, oder was?

...guudie, sischer häng' isch noch an der Mauer.
es wor ja nisch olles schleschd...
un immer wieder gob es eine unerwordede Froide.

...na wie? kleigorierdes Gästschendängen,
in den Fufzgern steh'ngebliebn?
Sie gönn' mir mol'n Buggel runderrudschn!

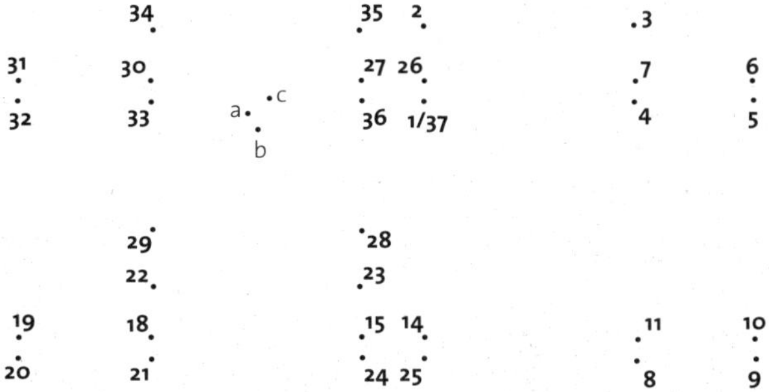

34

35 2

.3

31 30

32 33

a .c

b

27 26

7 6

4 5

36 1/37

29

22

28

23

19 18

20 21

15 14

24 25

11 10

8 9

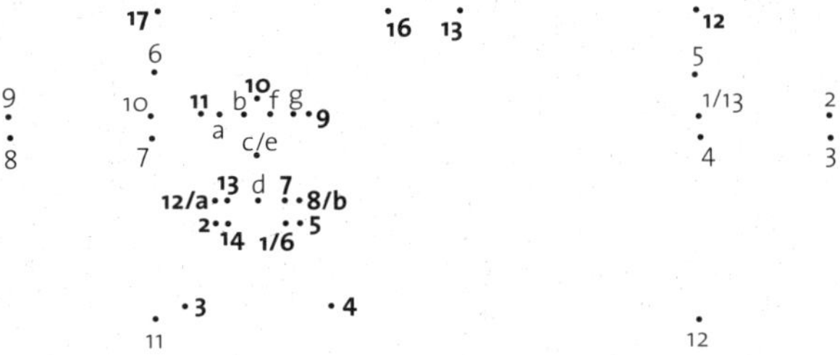

17

6

16 13

12

5

9

10 11 b .10 f g

a

7 c/e 9

1/13

2

4 3

8

12/a 13 d 7 8/b

2 14 1/6 5

3 4

11

12

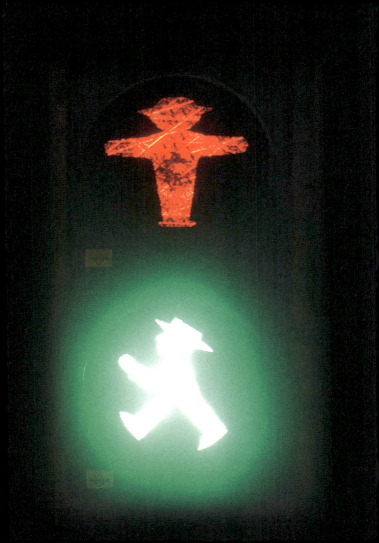

Erika verstaut alles, was in einer Kaffee- bzw. Teeküche gebraucht wird, an der Wand. Nichts wird versteckt. Die farbigen Paneele sind in 23 unterschiedliche Module, z.B. für Löffel, Tassen, Kaffee- bzw. Teekochen, Bevorratung oder Spülen aufgeteilt. Ein weiteres Paneel dient als Klapptisch. Wandpaneel FU (Sperrholz, Birke), Lamina t rot hochglänzend, FU (Sperrholz, Birke), schwarz, FU (Sperrholz, Birke), weiß. Halterung Edelstahl. Wand-Schiene Stahlblech, warmgewalzt.

'Erika' stashes everything you need for a small kitchen directly on the wall. Nothing is concealed. Coloured panels are divided into individual modules, each designed for a specific use. Spoons, mugs, crystal glasses, a coffee maker, an electric kettle for a hot cup of tea...a place for everything and everything in its place. Other kitchen tools or utensils for washing up can be stored away too. And there is a fold-away panel that is also a coffee table. Wall panel FU (birch plywood), laminate, red gloss. FU (birch plywood), black. FU (birch plywood), white. Racks, stainless steel. Wall mounted rails, sheet steel, plated.

Erika Storno 2005 Paneele/*panels* h/h 29/62/95 b/w 29/62 t/d variabel/*variable*, max. 31 (Tisch/*table* t/d 116,8), Schienen/*rails* h/h 3 I 66/99/165 t/d 1,9

pas de bourée / / / / /

en avant! / /   /
/   /   /   /   /
de coté

/ / /   /   /   / / /   /

effacé / / / /
en face /   / / / *ecarté derrière*

coupé   / / / /

4

3/34

27 · 31/33
30 ·

5 ·   23   26 ·
9 6 · 10   ·
13   1 2 15 !9
12   14/18 22
21   25 · ·24   ·32

29 · ·28

·11

8 · ·7   · 20

17 · ·16

Der Tisch verbindet filigrane Leichtigkeit mit hoher Stabilität und Belastbarkeit. Die flexible Tischplatte aus nur 9 mm starkem Birkensperrholz gewährleistet auch auf unebenen Untergründen einen festen Stand. Beistell-, Sitz- und Steh-höhe. Platte: Linoleum in rot, blau oder schwarz, FU (Sperrholz, Birke) natur klarlackiert, mit lackiertem Ahornfurnier oder mit Laminatoberflächen in den Farben: rot, blau, gelb, grau und weiß. Beine: FU (Sperrholz, Birke) natur geölt, schwarz.

This table combines a graceful and light design with a high degree of stability. The flexible table top made of 9 mm birch plywood guarantees that it stands firm on uneven surfaces, too. The legs of 'Spanoto' are available in three different heights: seated, standing, and coffee table. Table top, linoleum red, blue or black; FU (birch plywood) natural, clear varnish or varnished maple. Surface laminate, red, blue, yellow, grey or white. Legs, FU (birch plywood) oiled, black.

Spanoto   Jakob Gebert   1997   t/*d* 86   b/*w* 86/160/190/220

Ich kann das Wort „Outlet" nicht mehr hören ...

... nein, ich meine Haute Couture, das ist eben nicht wie Prêt-à-porter, wissen Sie ...
Vor allen Dingen sind auch die Marken wichtig, nein, bitte kein Secondhand,
auch nicht zweite Wahl, bitte.

... Nein, keine Pelze, also bitte.

(flüstert) Ich jogge doch so gerne nackt ...

3̲ 4̲ 7̲ 8̲ 11 12

bc fg jk

BCFG J K

1/17•   2 5 6 9 10 13   •14
        a d e h i l
18•   •16/1   A D E H I   •15/21
      •19/2   •20

Eine beliebig wählbare Anzahl von Stäben steckt lose in einem quadratischen Sockel und bildet so eine Garderobe, in der ein „Durchblättern" der Stangen möglich ist. Sie kann durch Stäbe mit verschiedenen Funktionen erweitert werden: als Schirmständer (Pin Brolly), als Leitsystem (Pin Flag) oder Leuchte (Pin Light). Sockel Zementguss weiß-grau. Stäbe Esche unbehandelt oder Nussbaum geölt.

With 'Pin Coat', a number of rods are inserted into the square base to create a coat rack. The rods can be jiggled to new positions. Other rods turn the unit into an umbrella stand (Pin Brolly), a navigation system (Pin Flag) or a lamp (Pin Light). Base, cement-cast, white-grey. Rods, untreated ash or oiled walnut.

Pin Coat   Oliver Bahr   2002   Sockel/*base* h/*h* 6 b/t, *w/d* 39,3/29
Stäbe/*rods* h/*h* 170/130/90 b/t, *w/d* 2,5

Dienen ist passion, not only profession ...

Der Niedergang des Empire? Das habe ich jetzt nicht gehört ...
... sicher gab es bessere Zeiten, well...

Hello Sir, yes please, Mr. Gestalter, *Times New Roman please!*
Na bitte, man muss auf alles achten.

... nicht einmal war ich krank, nicht in 30 Jahren ...
Urlaub? Sie scherzen!
(hüstelt) ... natürlich ... das ist eine Lebensaufgabe,
aber ich bin glücklich.

Die Bügelfalte ist eine Kunst, die leider vom Aussterben
bedroht ist ...

2

•2/1

4/c
1•   •5

3/15
3/A •   13/17
16• • ••12

21/B • 14/20

                              b.•

                    •a
              B.

    •a

  b. .A

                    7/d• •6

                •11
                10
                •9

4• •6   •8
  5

  7• •19/24
  22 23
  18

Dresscode bietet Platz nicht nur für das ‚Kleine Schwarze'. Man kann ihn drehen und wenden wie man will, er macht – auch als Raumteiler – immer eine gute Figur. Die Wände sind in einem Rahmen aus Eschenholz fixiert und bestehen aus einem neuartigen Textilverbundmaterial. Das Innenleben von Dresscode lässt sich individuell mit Fachböden und Kleiderstangen ausgestalten. Außenseite rot, olivgrün, grau, Innenseite schwarz.

'Dresscode' offers space, not only for your evening gown. It can be turned and rotated as you wish and makes a great room divider. The side panels – held in an ash frame – are made from a new compound fabric, a thermal manufacturing process ensuring stability. Its inner world can be individually designed, using various shelves and clothes rails. Outer fabric red, olive-green, grey. Inner fabric, black.

Dresscode Jörg Boner 2004 h/*h* 202 b/*w* 61/122 t/*d* 61

—» La mer ~

       qu'on voit danser
         lelong des golfes claire
a des reflects d'argent ~

                           la mer ~
ses blancs moutons. Avec les anges si purs ~~

~ la mer
       qu'on voit danser
       lelong des golfes claire

a des reflects d'argent ~

                     la mer«—

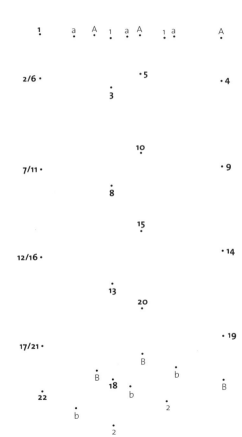

Ein Regal darf nicht wackeln? Es ist nicht starr, aber stabil, steht zu seinem Bewegungsdrang und funktioniert trotzdem. Von allen Seiten zugänglich, fällt nichts aus Es heraus. Wie Sie Es auch wackeln, bleiben die Regalebenen horizontal und sind hoch belastbar. Stangen: Buche massiv. Böden: Buchensperrholz unbehandelt.

Who said shelves shouldn't wobble? 'Es' is not stiff, but stable. It remains true to its urge to move, but functions like a dream. Although accessible from all sides, nothing ever falls out. Whichever way the shelves are wobbled they remain flat and can bear heavy loads. Rods, solid beech. Boards, beech plywood, untreated.

Es Konstantin Grcic 1998 h/*h* 141 b/*w* 60 t/*d* 40 lichte Fachhöhe/*compartment height* 34

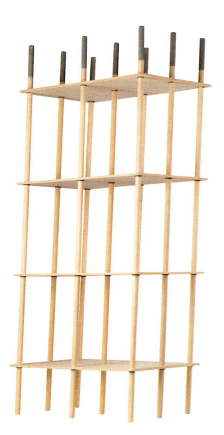

(Imaginärer Beifall)

... darf ich Sie ganz herzlich begrüßen, hier an diesem denkwürdigen, ja bedeutsamen und – wenn Sie so wollen – unvergleichlichen Ort.

Es ist mir eine ganz besondere Freude, dass und dass ausgerechnet an diesem Tag wir – und wenn ich von wir spreche, dann wissen Sie, dass ich schon immer und auch wiederholt gesagt habe, dass das 'wir' auch in Zukunft eine immer größere Rolle spielen wird. Darüber hinaus sehe ich in den anstehenden Aufgaben auch eher große Chancen, gerade und nicht zuletzt, weil diese – und das habe ich immer gesagt und sage es auch noch einmal – nicht an erster Stelle stehen. Das sind ja gerade die Aufgaben, denen wir uns heute stellen und auch immer gestellt haben. Ich sage es noch einmal. Nach vorne sehen, das ist es, was auch morgen und in Zukunft von Bedeutung ist, die nicht zuletzt genau so – und das meine ich so, wie ich es hier in aller Deutlichkeit sage. Ich kann das auch gerne noch einmal wiederholen. Ich sage es noch einmal, ... ich danke Ihnen für Ihre Aufmerksamkeit –

– ich muss weg!

3· ·2

4/17· ·1 16·

5· 13· ·6 ·14

10· ·9

·15

8· ·7

12· ·11

Ein filigranes und handliches Stehpult, das an nahezu jede Wand und jedes Bücherregal angelehnt werden kann. Durch das Anbringen eines dritten Standbeins kann Der kleine Lehner auch frei im Raum stehen. Board FU (Sperrholz, Birke) weiß oder schwarz, oder beidseitig laminierte Oberfläche rot/gelb, blau/grau oder schwarz/weiß. Beine: Esche massiv, unbehandelt oder Nussbaum geölt.

A gracefully designed and handy writing stand, which can be leant against almost any wall or shelf. And with a third leg, it becomes possible to place 'Der kleine Lehner' wherever needed in the room. Board, either FU (birch plywood), white or black, or double-sided laminate surface in red/yellow, blue/grey or black/white. Legs, solid ash, untreated, or oiled walnut.

Der kleine Lehner Jörg Gätjens 2003 h/*h* 107 b/*w* 45 t/*d* 45/52

Habt ihr schon die Neuen gesehen? Seh'n ja teuer aus ...

> *wo?*
> *wo?*
> *wo?*
> *wo?*

... hat sie angeblich vom Ex bekommen ... diesem Stinkstiefel!

> *ach was?*
> *ach was?*
> *ach was?*
> *ach was?*

... was soll man da sagen?

> *Das gibt Ärger, das rieche ich.*
> *Das gibt Ärger, das rieche ich.*
> *Das gibt Ärger, das rieche ich.*
> *Das gibt Ärger, das rieche ich.*

3 • • 2/8   4 • 34 • 33   • 32
    • 7   • 1 • 2
    • 6

5 •

a •   • 3

b •   6 •   • 9   • 7
10 •

A •   • 8

15 • B • 11 •   • 14   • 12

a •   • 13

20 • b • 16 •   • 17
                    • 19

A •   • 18

25 • B • 21 •   • 22
                    • 24

a •

    • d   • 23

b • • 26 •
    c   27 • • 30   • 31
    4 • • • 5   28 • • 29/35
        1

Durch den Kippmechanismus werden alle Fächer der Schuhkippe gleichzeitig geöffnet oder geschlossen. Lüftung und Reinigungsmöglichkeiten sind optimal. Sie bietet viel Stauraum bei minimalem Platzbedarf. Für zehn Paar Schuhe angeboten bis Schuhgröße 43. Pulverbeschichtetes Stahlblech in verschiedenen Farbkombinationen.

The tilting mechanism serves to open and close all compartments simultaneously. The shoe hopper offers maximum storage capacity while taking up only a minimum amount of space. 'Schuhkippe' is wide enough for ten pairs of shoes and takes shoe-size maximum 9 (UK). Powder-coated steel sheet in a number of colour combinations.

Schuhkippe   Hanspeter Weidmann   1984   h/*h* 165   b/*w* 53   t/*d* 16

Also mal ehrlich, der Einzige, der hier keine Macke hat und fest mit beiden Beinen auf der Erde steht, bin ich.

Ich bin so normal, so solide.
Ich frage mich ehrlich, was ich hier soll ...

Ich sehe mich ja eher in einem großen SB-Mitnahme-Möbelhaus ...

h i f/j
b• •• •
  C c/g

G • • B/D/H

I/1
•

6
5/11 • • • 1/7/a
4/8/12

13 • • A

•
a

F • • • J
E/K

2 • • e
d/3

10 • • • b
9/c

14 • • 2
3/15

Eine Edelstahlzarge verbindet jeweils zwei Beine zu einer einfachen aber robusten Konstruktion. Durch die Flexibilität des Stahlblechs berühren alle Fußpunkte auch auf unebenen Untergründen den Boden und gewährleisten einen stabilen Stand. Beine gewachste, schwarz gebeizte oder klarlackierte Buche.

A stainless steel frame joins two pairs of legs in a simple yet stable combination. The flexibility of the steel sheet allows all four feet to touch the floor, even on irregular surfaces, and ensures that the construction is stable. Legs, solid beech, waxed, black glaze or clear varnish.

Taurus Jörg Sturm, Susanne Wartzeck 1993 h/*h* 72 b/*w* 37 t/*d* 71,6

Sie ziehen sich erst bitte eine Nummer. Jeder muss sich eine NUMMER ziehen! Auch, wenn Sie ganz alleine sind. Bevor wir hier irgendetwas anfangen, zieht jeder erst mal eine Nummer.

Und *RUHE!!* Der Haufen da hinten regt mich schon den ganzen Morgen auf. Meine Philosophie ist 33, 67,6, 34, 50. Sie glauben ja gar nicht, in was man alles eine Ordnung bringen kann.

(((=)))

Und hört jetzt auf so zu **schieben**, es kommen alle aufs Bild!

2 ··1/29	26 ··25	22 ··21	18·17
··28	27 ··24	23 ··20	19·
d	c ·4	3 ·D	C
·a	b ··1	2 ··A	B·
h	g ·8	7 ·H	G
·e	f ··5	6 ··E	F·
·l	k ··12	11 ··L	K·
·i	j ··9	10 ··l	J·
p	o ·16	15 ·P	O
·m	n ··13	14 ··M	N·
·t	s ··20	19 ··T	S·
·q	r ··17	18 ··Q	R·
·x	w ··24	23 ··X	W·
·u	v ··21	22 ··U	V·
·5	6 ··9	10 ··13	14·
3 ··4	7 ··8	11 ··12	15 ··16

Als reine Struktur ist das Regal reduziert auf Wangen und Böden, die im Verbund mit den eingesteckten Aluminium-Schienen die Transparenz des Entwurfs in den Vordergrund stellen. FNP ist nachträglich erweiterbar und ohne Werkzeug aufzubauen. MDF natur klarlackiert, schwarz gewachst, braun gewachst, rot gewachst, pastellblau, pastellgrün, orange, rot, weiß, grau, schwarz, FU (Sperrholz, Birke) weiß, schwarz.

The design of this shelving system has been reduced to side panels and shelves. When joined by aluminium rails these elements accentuate the transparency of the structure itself. FNP can be extended at any time. No tools are needed to assemble FNP. Either MDF natural clear varnish, black waxed, brown waxed, red waxed, light blue, light green, orange, red, white, grey, black, or FU (birch plywood), white, black.

FNP Axel Kufus 1989 h/*h* 103,2/223/259,6/332,8 b/*w* 33/67,6 t/*d* 34/50

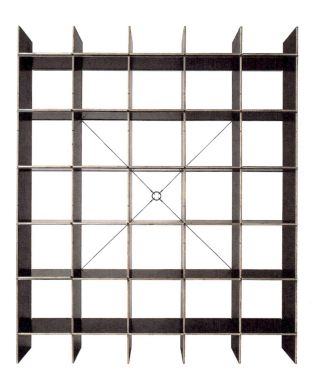

FNP Bibliotheksleiter h/h 265,4 b/w 37,3 t/d 7,4/ca. 85

Rosi Lamp h/h 44,5 b/w 8 t/d 17
FNP Stehpult h/h 7,7 FNP: b/w 33/67,7 t/d 35,5
FNP X: b/w 23/48 t/d 27,0
FNP Fix für Fächer/*for compartments* h/h 34,7 b/w 33/67,7
FNP Wenig h/h 5,3 b/w 6,2 t/d 20
FNP Boxen h/h 10,8/21,6/32,5 b/w 32,5 t/d 34
FNP Ablagebox, Stehsammler, Hängeregistratur

FNP X *(nicht im Bild)*
h/h 103,2/223/259,6/332,8 b/w 23,2/48 t/d 21/34
lichte Fachhöhen/*compartment heights* 4,2/10,3/16,4/22,5/28,6/34,7

Hallo …

             … ICH BIN HIER OBEN …

                      Haalloo …

        JA   SIEHT MICH   DENN keiner?
                         Ich bin das Alpenglühn!!!

Haallo!   *Hier im Aktenordner!*

                        Haaaaaaaallllllloooo! Holadio ladio …

2/a
3 ·
19 ·
· 1/20

14 ·   22   21
       ·   ·   · 13
       16/23   12/17
15 ·   · 11

18 ·

4 ·   7   8   9
        ·   ·   ·
            6   · 10
        ·
        5/b

Ladio ladio ...

Ladio ladio ...

Schlicht ist eine Leuchte im Ordnerformat, die vor allem für die Verwendung in Regalen entworfen wurde. Durch den mittels einer beweglichen Blende verstellbaren Lichtaustritt und einen flexiblen Schalter kann sie in unterschiedlichen Höhen im Regal ihren Platz finden. Die Rückwand der Leuchte besteht aus transluzentem Acrylglas, verfügbar in den Farben: glas-look satiniert, rot, orange, blau und grün. Aluminium eloxiert.

'Schlicht' is a shelf light designed in the shape of a file. With its adjustable plate and remote switching, light emerges wherever necessary and 'Schlicht' can be used at various heights in a shelf. Rear surface, translucent plexiglass, glass-look satin, red, orange, blue, green. Aluminium anodised.

Schlicht BFGF, Büro für Gestaltungsfragen 2002 h/*h* 32 b/*w* 10,5 t/*d* 21

ladio ...

(leise flüsternd)

...wir haben gesündigt...

...auf den Boden getropft,
mit Wachs gekleckert, gezündelt, an die Decke gerußt,
Brandgeruch verbreitet...
und dann...
...aber das haben wir gar nicht gewollt...

Jetzt haben wir Ihnen alles gebeichtet
und Sie sprechen von gespaltenen Persönlichkeiten!

Wie, cholerisch? **Paartherapie?**
Ich mach Dir gleich Feuer...

14
13 15
11 12 16
9 10 17 18

a/d b

8 c 19
7 20
6 21

4/1 5 22 23/3
1/2

3 24
2/25

Zwei Winkeleisen in einem Fundament aus Beton, eingeschlossen in einen Stahlkubus – die skulptural anmutenden Kerzenleuchter halten Kerzen jeder Größe und Form durch das einfache Prinzip der Klemmung.

Two angle-irons in a concrete base, enclosed by a steel cube, these candlesticks turned sculpture hold candles of any size and shape by clamping them securely.

Viktor & Viktoria Fauxpas 1990 Viktor h/*h* 50 Viktoria h/*h* 158

Prinzipiell ist diese Art der Komplexität, welche sich durch Verbindungen und Verschachtelungen, auch dann deutlich in der Unterscheidbarkeit, die temporär wie imaginär durch Stabilität und Exaktheit, strukturiert und gleichzeitig senkrecht wie waagerecht gespannt, in jeglicher Höhe auch hoch oben, und zugleich, was nicht weniger wichtig ist, sich auszeichnend durch extreme Ästhetik und Klarheit, überaus spannend im Detail und insgesamt doch sehr bewundernswert.
Also mal unter uns, ich frage mich immer, wie das hält?

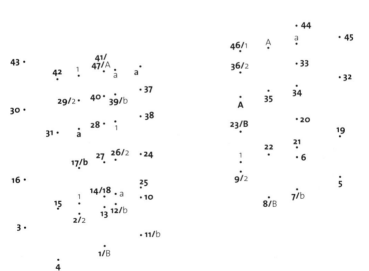

43 •

41/
47/A
a
42 1
a
29/2 40 39/b
30 •
31 • 28 1
a
27 26/2 •24
17/b
16 •
25
14/18 •a
15 1 •10
13 12/b
2/2
3 •
•11/b
1/B
4

37
•38

•44
46/1 A a •45
36/2 •33
•32
34
A 35
23/B •20
19
22 21
1 •6
9/2
5
8/B 7/b

Sideboard, Bücherregal oder Ablage. Das System ist vielseitig. Funktional und flexibel können die Module jederzeit einfach umgebaut oder beliebig erweitert werden. Die abgekanteten Tablare haben die Form von Schienen. In diese können Boxen in vier Richtungen eingesteckt werden. Auf ihnen ruht dann wiederum das nächste Tablar. Aluminium eloxiert.

Sideboard, book-case, or filing cabinet this is a versatile system. Functional and flexible, the modules can be rearranged or expanded at any time. The rounded front of the boards contain grooves into which boxes can be placed to face in four different directions. These boxes also support the next shelf. Aluminium anodised.

Zoll D   Lukas Buol, Marco Zünd   1993

Boxen/*boxes* h/*h* 16/22/33/44
Tablare/*panels* b/*w* 99/143/160/190/220 t/*d* 33

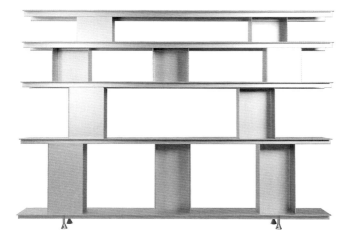

Seit längerem werde
ich kurz gehalten
und bin ganz schön
abgemagert ...

... angeblich bin ich
unbeweglich geworden ...

Jaa, früher hing ich
noch gut im Futter,
was ham sich alle
um mich gekloppt.

– dengel, dengel, boing boing –

Ja, sehr witzig, was?
... wie sehe ich denn
jetzt aus?

9/11/13
•

7/10 •   •12   2/8•   •3/14

a •   °   •b

A•   °   •B

a •   °   •b

•6   °   •1/5   •4

Der Container wächst von oben nach unten und berührt somit den Boden nicht. Die eingehängten Türen schließen selbsttätig durch ihr Eigengewicht. Zur Gliederung der einzelnen Elemente werden zusätzlich spezielle Fachunterteilungen angeboten. Abgekantetes Stahlblech, verzinkt oder Stahlblech silber- oder orange-feinstruktur pulverbeschichtet.

The container was designed from the top down, so that it does not touch the floor. The doors hang on hinges and close automatically by their own weight. For easier storage, partitions are available. Steel sheet, galvanised clear or powder-coated, silver or orange.

Hängecontainer Marcus Botsch 1989 5 Elemente/*elements* h/*h* 210 b/*w* 34 t/*d* 34

Ja, ich weiss, es sieht sehr leicht aus...
Neulich hatte ich einen, der hat es eine ganze Stunde lang probiert...

Dann ist er rausgegangen und hat Holz gehackt.

9
.8

12 .11

14.
15:

13. 1/10   5
. 7 .4   :
16 :   6
2: a d
3

b c

Trick Stick besteht aus drei Stäben, die nach traditioneller japanischer Holzverbindung ohne Werkzeug zusammengesteckt werden. So entsteht eine Ablage für Hüte, Schals und Jacken. Trick Stick steht lässig auf einem Bein, lehnt an der Wand und kann, wenn er nicht gebraucht wird, platzsparend verstaut werden. Stäbe Esche massiv. Rutschstop Silikon. Die drei Stab-Enden sind in den Farben weiß, rot und blau lackiert.

Für alle, die Trick Stick nicht auf die Schliche kommen: die Anleitung zur Knobel-Verbindung wird mitgeliefert.

Trick Stick is made of three sticks, joined without tools, and using a traditional Japanese technique. A place for hats, scarves and jackets is created. Trick Stick stands nonchalantly on one leg, leans on the wall and can be stowed away when not needed. Rods, solid ash. Sliding stop, silicone. Rod ends coated white, red and blue.

Assembly information included for all those unable to solve the Trick Stick puzzle.

Trick Stick Patrick Frey, Markus Boge 2005 Garderobe/*coat rack* h/*h* 155 b/*w*, t/*d* 51
Stäbe einzeln/*rods* l 155/51 b/*w*, t/*d* 1,5

                                Pling
                fünfter Stock, SB-Restaurant

                                Pling
                vierter Stock, Spielwaren

                                Pling
                dritter Stock, Haushaltswaren

                                Pling
                zweiter Stock, Herrenbekleidung

                                Pling
(Frauenstimme,   *erster Stock, Damenoberbekleidung*
gedämpfte Kaufhausmusik)

26/28
27/a · · 2

29
b · ·
3

25 ·

24/30
22/c · · 23

a ·

b ·

∘

·

∘

· c

A ·

B ·

∘

·

∘

· C

a ·

b ·

·

· c

A ·

·

B ·

·

· C

a ·

·

·

·

b ·

·

· c

A ·

·

B ·

∘

·

∘

· C

a ·

b ·

·

· c

A ·

·

6 · 1/5
7 · ·
8 ·
11 ·

B ·

·

·

· C
·

21/2

9 · 10 ·

4/1
12 · · 15

16 · · · 20
19

13 · · 14

17 · 18

Das Baukastensystem besteht aus Schubkästen und Korpuselementen in vier
Höhen, die beliebig übereinander ange-
ordnet werden können. Durch Drehen
der Schubkastenblende kann die Front-
ansicht individuell gestaltet werden:
Auf der einen Seite befindet sich ein
einzelnes Griffloch, auf der anderen zwei
zusätzliche Löcher. FU (Sperrholz, Birke)
natur klarlackiert, weiß, schwarz. Zusätzlich Material Deckplatte: Linoleum rot,
blau oder schwarz.

*This modular system consists of drawers
and frame elements (in four sizes) which
can be arranged in any combination. The
drawers have two different fronts. One
front has a single finger hole, the other has
two additional holes. Drawer fronts viewed
by turning. FU (birch plywood), natural,
clear varnish, white, black. Additional
material (top), linoleum red, blue, black.*

Lader Axel Kufus 1996 h/*h* variabel/*variable* b/*w* 44,2/83,2/122/161 t/*d* 51
Schübe/*drawers* h/*h* 7,1/10,8/14,6/29,5

... ja natürlich kann man auch auf mir sitzen, was soll die Frage?

(---|| ||| ||| |)

Ich finde, man bleibt ja manchmal hinter seinen Möglichkeiten ...

(---|| ||| ||| |)

Auf den ersten Blick könnte man mit einem Steinway ja auch Boot fahren.

(---|| ||| ||| |)

Aber ich brauche das Publikum ...

(---|| ||| ||| |)

... die Atmosphäre ...

(---|| ||| ||| |--- ||||)

Hören Sie mir überhaupt zu?

(---|| ||| ||| |)

2

1/5

3/19

B

4/20

b

7   8   c   d   A
6   e
1/9 b   f   B
5   a
2   a/i g
h   b
4   3   A
D   E
C   F   B
a
B   G   A   b
6   8
7   A/K H   a   B
J   I
9   A   16 18
17
10   15
11   14
12/21 13

Die vier Seiten des Kleinen Trommlers sind als unterschiedliche Perkussionsflächen ausgebildet und ermöglichen ungeahnte Klangbilder. FU (Sperrholz, Birke) weiß, schwarz, natur klarlackiert.

The four sides of 'Kleiner Trommler' (Little Drummer) are designed as individual percussive surfaces and enable unique sounds to be produced. FU (birch plywood), natural clear varnish, white, black.

Kleiner Trommler   Clemens Stübner, Sabine Mrasek   2001   h/*h* 47   b/*w* 46   t/*d* 46

Jaa leck mi ... host du den Oarsch g'seng?

Ja so einen Oarsch findst du in ganz Bayern ned.

Ja, do legst di nieda! I glaab mia brennt da Huat. Ja so a Blunz'n!

Oarschlings schaut's mi o! Jaa jetzt –

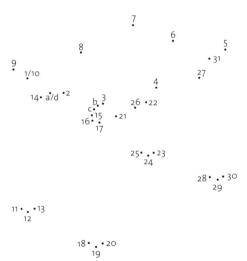

7

6

5

8   ·31
9   27
1/10
                4
14· a/d ·2
        b 3
        c ·15   26· ·22
16·   ·21
17
        25· ·23
        24
              28· ·30
              29
11· ·13
12
18· ·20
19

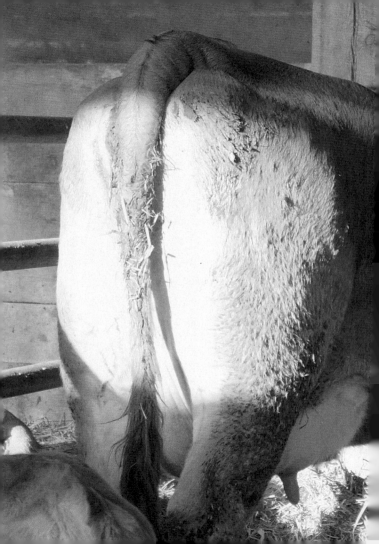

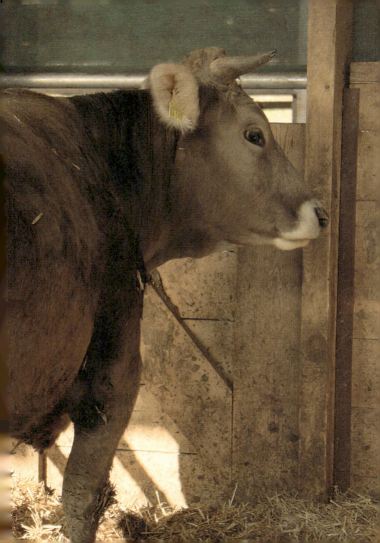

Sitzmichl ist ein Falthocker, braucht nur einen winzigen Platz in der Ecke und hält die Klappe. Beim Aufklappen entsteht eine bequeme, gewölbte Sitzfläche, in der die Beine genial einfach und stabil fixiert sind. Sitzfläche FU (Sperrholz, Birke) schwarz beschichtet. Beine Esche unbehandelt.

'Sitzmichl' is a folding stool, one which requires very little space in the corner. It tends to keep its trap shut! A comfortable, curved seat appears on opening the stool. The legs are mounted in a simple and stable way. Seat FU (birch plywood), black. Legs, ash, untreated.

Sitzmichl Jacob Müller 1948 Neuinterpretation/*new interpretation* Nils Holger Moormann 2004
h/*h* 47 b/*w* 53,6 t/*d* 40

Were you ever in New York?
On top of the Empire State?
That's what I feel like every morning.
No sooner have I opened my eyes than I think:
"Whatever you do, don't look down.
Whatever you do, don't look down."
So what do I do? Naturally, I look down!
And already I feel faint; my heart races
And I've gone all weak at the knees.
In my job of course,
Being afraid of heights is fatal!

What I mean is,
How many people are going to trust me
If they find out that I'm afraid of heights?
One thing's for sure, I work at it each day,
And I do believe it's got a little better.

What I need is someone to lean on,
A dependable partner at my side,
If you know what I mean.

Have you discovered what it really means to be slow? I think I can help with the definition. I'm **"Last minute"**, by the way. And I just love spontaneity, the sense of speed, adapting myself to new situations…and Moormann goes and opens a shop in *Bern* of all places! I suppose he thinks I'm going to go down well in this country. What makes things worse, I have this terrible fear of failure. My brother in Vienna tells me it's the same there.

Don't be taken in by my plain appearance. I just know there's something of enormous import deep inside me. It seems you're someone to be envied, now that you've made my acquaintance. Sit down for a little while and savour this incredible moment. Believe me, the two of us would make a great winning team. Just imagine the headlines! We'd make it in the papers around the world. Victory is ours.

For I am an island, for I am an island, for I am an island–

For I am an island, for I
am an island, for I am an island –
For I am an island,
(reads: hmm…Miller, Hesse, Freud—Freud???…)
…for I am an island, for I am an island.

Never, never, never ever!

   ...b u t...

The book has no poetic soul. And the author is completely overrated.

   ... ...

   ...Perhaps I might just intervene here...

...completely over...

   Fine, the author is completely...

And where is the eroticism? Nonexistant I would have thought.

   On the other hand –

It bores me to tears...

   That's far too much of a generalisation.

   ...but the typescript...

...I don't read typescripts, never, NEVER EVER!!

   (slowly starts to rotate)

Call me what you will, ▬▬▬▬▬▬▬▬▬▬▬▬
Why don't you just go and f___ off! It's, like, so f___▬▬▬▬...
So who the f___ understands? Up, down, in, out ▬▬▬▬▬
Do what the f___ you want!

(A female voice with a cute French accent)
Merde! The same wretched dream every night. It just keeps on coming back.
Exactly. Again and again. I am falling. And I keep falling and falling. Down and down I go.
And land on a sweet little dog! Again and again.
Non, up to now everything has been fine in the morning.

Would you know it, just looking at me you'd never guess how much sound I can produce...but there's never anyone around to play with me...
Stuff and nonsense. Of course you can play everything you want on a single string. Sound emanates from the body of course. Have you ever played a minuet with handkerchiefs and half-full bottles of shampoo? Give it a try. Come on, have a go!

In Your world a boundless chaos rules.
You think of me as but bent
and buckled wood?
And yet I think, therefore I am!

I long for rationality,
Recognition in its purest form,
The object is a banality,
To postulate world order, the norm.

Shall I stare into the distant haze
Vision obscured by adumbrate cloud?
There doth ripen many a phrase
That will be heard out loud.

Return to ponderous and weighty sense,
Whisper feeble voices in my ear.
To overcome without pretence,
I ne'er shall sacrifice a tear.

These are lines to serve my mind
That worm t'wards paper from the quill.
Like forfeit treasure, hard to find,
Thoughts exhibit a special will.

Reason, reason; shall any suit?
And whether sense be cloyed,
Primordial matter lies in dispute,
But the transcendental is void.
(...leaves...)

Unsullied meaning, vivid and clear,
Th' immortal state to gain.
Read! Live! Hold no fear,
Gain awareness without pain.

See, he leaveth, and so it proves
That way unfolds insanity,
For all the intelligence that moves,
Transcendence remains but a vanity.

Who may I say is calling? Do you have an *appointment*? I'm
terribly sorry. *Without* one I could not ***possibly*** apprise anyone of
your presence. Now don't get iffy with me, for all I know, you
could be *anybody*…Right, time to leave I think, and don't forget
your hat and coat, I am ***not*** your personal cloakroom.

(When the moon has overcome twice the sun,
Bury my heart where the river bends.
Does the white man, who needs a shrink to talk,
Have something to cure homesickness?)

Is it all right if I lean on you? The fear of being left alone. You're a one.
But are you not afraid of being on your own? I need a strong partner.
I'm nothing on my own. I simply have to lean up against someone.
When did all this begin?

(With a broad East German accent)
So how can you tell I come from the other side?
Is it written all over my face or what?
I'm still attached to the wall, not all of it was bad.
Happiness came along unexpectedly. What?
Petty-minded pigeonhole thinking, stuck in the 1950s?
Nuts to you!

I simply can't hear the word "outlet" ever again.
Sorry, but I was referring to haute couture. That's not the same
as prêt à porter, as I'm sure you must realise. The main thing is,
to get the right labels. And please, no second hand, and no
seconds either, Pur-lease!

...And no, no furs either. Pur-lease!
(Whispered) I love to go jogging in my birthday suit.

To serve is a passion, not only a profession...
The decline and fall of the British Empire?
I for one will not hear of it. Of course, we did enjoy better times...
Hello Sir, yes please, Mr. Typesetter, *Times New Roman please!*
You have to think of everything these days. And never once was I ill,
Not once in thirty years. A holiday? I assume you are joking!
(Clearing his throat) Well, that is my life for you.
But I must say that I am happy. Ironing a crease is quite an art:
One threatened with extinction I am reluctant to say.

(A wobbling bookcase sings an old French folk song)
»*Somewhere over the sea ~She's there waiting for me ~ ~*
~ ~ ~ ~ My lover stands on golden sands ... «—

(Imaginary applause) Hello! And a very warm welcome to all who have
gathered here today at such an impressive and, well, most auspicious
spot. There is – if I may say so – nowhere quite like it. May I say right away
that it gives me great pleasure to note that today is the very day on
which we – and when I say we, please don't forget the many occasions on
which I said this, for it is something I have always stood for, that it is "we"
who will play a growing role in the future. In the great crusade that lies
before us, I can see even greater opportunities, if only for the very good
reason – and this I have said in the past and will say again now – that
these are simply not going to stand in our way. For it is these very tasks,
ones that we must address today and which in the past we have always
addressed. Let me reiterate. Look to the future, for that is what tomorrow
is, and all our tomorrows too, if only because that is how things always
turn out. Let me emphasise at this point – and in the clearest way
possible. Once again, I am only too glad to recapulate. So let me just say
this one last time...both in a final sense and in the broadest possible
terms. Thank you for your attention ... Sorry, I really have to leave!

Seen the new ones then? Look rather dear to me.
　　　　Where? Where? Where? Where?
Got them from her "ex" apparently. And they stink to high heaven!
　　　　No, really? No, really? No, really? No, really?
What can one do?
　　　　Bound to cause trouble, you can smell it a mile away. (4x)

To be honest, the only one who's normal around here and has
Both feet planted firmly on the ground, that's me.
I really am very normal, solidly built, if you want to put it that way.
But I have to ask myself, what on earth am I doing here?
I see myself more in one of those huge DIY stores on the roundabout.

(quietly, whispering)
　　　　　　　　...for we have sinned... dripped on the floor,
splashed wax, played with fire, left soot on the ceiling,
　　　　　　　spread the stench of fire
...and then...　　　　but this is not what we did not wish for.
　　　Now that we have confessed everything to you,
　　　All you can talk about are split personalities!
　　　What do you mean, choleric? **Partner therapy!?**
　　　I'll give you fire if you want.

In principle, this kind of complexity, which in its own congruities, and
meandering phraseology, is also marked in its very differentiation,
evinces both in the temporal and imaginary senses a kind of stability
and exactness that simultaneously stretches across vertical and
horizontal parameters at any and each height, extending ever
upwards, too, whilst at the same time – and this is of no less impor-
tance – exhibiting through stark aesthetics and clarity of such
piquant detail that it is, taken in its entirety, something quite
amazing. If you ask me, and I do it a lot myself, I'd like to know how
the bloody thing stands up!

For a long time now I've been somewhat starved, and a shadow of my
former self. Apparently, I've been lacking exercise. I know, I used to be
quite staunch. Everyone punched me, it hardly bears thinking about.
　　　　–Thwack, thwack, thock, thock –
Ha ha! Very funny. My God, just look at me now!?

OK, I KNOW IT ALL LOOKS QUITE EASY.
ONLY LAST WEEK I HAD SOMEONE… TRIED A WHOLE HOUR.

IN THE END HE WENT OUTSIDE AND CHOPPED WOOD.

(Faint Muzak, anonymous female voice)
Ping!   First floor, Women's wear.
Ping!   Second floor, Men's wear.
Ping!   Third floor, Household goods.
Ping!   Fourth floor, Children's toys.
Ping!   The fifth floor self-service restaurant!

First you have to get a number. Everyone has to have a NUMBER!
(Just pull the tab downwards.) Even if you're on your own. So, before we do anything, lets see to it that all of you have a number.
SILENCE! The rabble at the back have been getting on nerves all
morning. My philosophy is 33, 67,6, 34, 50. You'd hardly believe
the number of things you can do with numbers.
          (((=)))
And stop **pushing**, you're all in the picture!

Hello!   …Here I am, UP HERE…
Hal-loo… CAN'T YOU SEE ME?   I'm the alpenglow.
Here in the file!   Haaaaaal-looooooo! Haal-looo…

Yes of course you can sit on me. What sort of a question is that?
(---|| ||| ||||)
If you ask me, one's full potential is never realised.
At first glance, you'd think you could sail away on a Steinway!
(---|| ||| ||||)
But what I need is an audience. Such a wonderful atmosphere.
Are you listening to anything I'm saying?
(---|| ||| ||| |--- ||||)

(In a marked Bavarian accent)
Lick my a*. Have you seen the a*** on that? You won't find an
a*** like that in the whole of Bavaria. You could knock me down
with a feather! I'm completely gobsmacked! It's ginormous!
She's looking at me! A***achingly amazing stuff.**

1543
Good Design Award, Chicago Athenæum 2000

Aktei
Auszeichnung für höchste Designqualität, „Die Besten der Besten', Designzentrum Nordrhein-Westfalen 1992 | Designauswahl, Design Center Stuttgart 1992 | The International Design Yearbook 93/94

Asket
Design Plus 1991

Billy Clever
interior innovation award cologne 2003, Kategorie best item | Internationaler Designpreis Baden-Württemberg 2003 Focus Balance in silber | Nominierung zum Designpreis Bundesrepublik Deutschland 2004 | The International Design Yearbook 2004

Der kleine Lehner
Internationaler Designpreis Baden-Württemberg 2004 Focus Dialog in silber | Deutscher Designer Club „Das gute Stück', Auszeichnung silber 2005

Di Mi Tri
Nominierung Designpreis Schweiz 2003

Dresscode
interior innovation award cologne 2005, Kategorie Best Material | Nominierung Designpreis Bundesrepublik Deutschland 2006 | Nominierung Designpreis Schweiz 2005 | Good Design Award, Chicago Athenæum 2005 | IF Product Design Award 2006 – Auszeichnung in Gold

Erika
Internationaler Designpreis Baden-Württemberg 2005 Focus Know How in silber

Es
Anerkennung Designpreis Schweiz 1999 | The International Design Yearbook 2000

Expander
Auszeichnung für hohe Designqualität, Design Zentrum Nordrhein-Westfalen 1993 | Anerkennung für herausragendes Produkt, Designpreis Schweiz 1993 | Auszeichnung für gutes Design, IF Hannover 1994

Egal
Good Design Award 2002, Chicago Athenæum | IF design award 2003 | Nominierung Designpreis Bundesrepublik Deutschland 2004

FNP
Auszeichnung für hohe Designqualität, Design Zentrum Nordrhein-Westfalen 1991 | Internationales Designjahrbuch 92/93 | md Auswahl die besten 200 für das Jahr 2000 | interior innovation award cologne 2003, Kategorie Classic Innovation

FNP X
IF Product Design Award 2001

Hängecontainer
Auszeichnung für hohe Designqualität, Designzentrum Nordrhein-Westfalen 1990

Hut ab
Blueprint 100% Design Award 1998 | The International Design Yearbook 1999

Kleiner Trommler
CNC-conForm 2001 höchste Auszeichnung | Good Design Award 2002, Chicago Athenæum | Internationaler Designpreis Baden-Württemberg 2002 Focus Lebensart in silber | IF Product Design Award 2003 | Nominierung Designpreis Bundesrepublik Deutschland 2004

Kant
Internationaler Designpreis Baden-Württemberg 2003 Focus Balance in silber | Lucky Strike junior award 2003 der Raymond Loewy Stiftung | Good Design Award 2003, Chicago Athenæum | Nominierung zum Designpreis Bundesrepublik Deutschland 2004 | The International Design Yearbook 2004 | Deutscher Designer Club „Das gute Stück', Auszeichnung Bronze 2005 | IF Product Design award 2005 | Nominierung Designpreis Bundesrepublik Deutschland 2006 | Prädikat: „Neuer Klassiker – die ersten 100 des 21. Jahrhunderts', Schöner Wohnen, 2005

Lader
The International Design Yearbook 97/98

Lamello
Design Center Stuttgart, Design Auswahl 1989

Last Minute
Design Plus 1993; Auszeichnung für hohe Designqualität, Design Zentrum Nordrhein Westfalen 1993 | Anerkennung für herausragendes Produkt, Design Preis Schweiz 1993 | Auszeichnung für gutes Design, IF Hannover 1994 | Deutscher Designer Club, DDC, Auszeichnung 1994 | Design Auswahl, Design Center Stuttgart 1994 | The International Design Yearbook 94/95

New Tramp
| Design Zentrum Nordrhein West-
falen, Auszeichnung für hohe
Designqualität 1994 | Design for
Europe, Kortrijk 1992

Pin Coat
| international furniture designfair
assahikawa,2002 | The International
Design Yearbook 2004 | Deutscher
Designer Club ,Das gute Stück',
Auszeichnung Bronze 2005 | Good
Design Award 2004, Chicago Athen-
næum | IF Product Design Award
2005 | Nominierung Designpreis
Bundesrepublik Deutschland 2006

Sitzmichl
| interior innovation award cologne
2005, Kategorie Classic Innovation
| Nominierung Designpreis Bundes-
republik Deutschland 2006

Soli
| Haus Industrieform Essen 1984

Spanoto
| Design for Europe 1996 3 x 1. Preis,
Kortrijk/Belgien | Top Ten ,Die Besten
der Besten', IF Hannover 1997
| Auszeichnung für hohe Design-
qualität, Design Zentrum Nordrhein
Westfalen 1997 | Anerkennung
commercial success, Internationaler
Designpreis des Landes Baden-
Württemberg 1997 | Bundespreis
Produktdesign 1998 | Interior innova-
tion award cologne 2004, Kategorie
Best System | interior innovation
award cologne 2004, Best of the best
in Kategorie Best System

Sparondo
| Internationaler Designpreis Baden-
Württemberg 2004 Focus Dialog in
silber

Step
| Anerkennung, Internationaler
Designpreis Baden-Württemberg
1997

Taurus
| Nürnberger Möbeldesign Kontakte
1993 | Auszeichnung für höchste
Designqualität, »Die Besten der Besten«, Design Zentrum Nordrhein-
Westfalen 1994 | Auszeichnung für
gutes Design, IF Hannover 1995
| Anerkennung für herausragendes
Produkt, Design Preis Schweiz 1995 |
md Auswahl die Besten 200 für das
Jahr 2000

Tischbocktisch
| Internationaler Designpreis Baden-
Württemberg Focus Arbeitswelten
2000 | Product Design Award des IF
2001 | Auszeichnung für hohe
Designqualität, Designzentrum
Nordrhein-Westfalen 2000
| Nominierung für den Designpreis
der Bundesrepublik Deutschland
2002

Viktor & Viktoria
| Design Plus 1991 | Auszeichnung
für hohe Designqualität, Design
Zentrum Nordrhein-Westfalen 1993

Zoll D
| Auszeichnung für höchste Design-
qualität, »Die Besten der Besten«
Design Zentrum Nordrhein-West-
falen 1994 | Deutscher Designer
Club, DDC, Silbermedaille 1994
| Auszeichnung für gutes Design
»Die Besten der Branche«, IF Hanno-
ver 1995 | Preis Design Preis Schweiz
1995 | Bundespreis Produktdesign
1996 | md Auswahl die besten für
das Jahr 2000

Moormann
| European Community Design Prize
1994; Auszeichnung für Innovation
in den Bereichen Designmanage-
ment, Produktgestaltung, visuelle
Kommunikation und Firmenarchi-
tektur | IF Hannover, Exhibition De-
sign Award, Silber, Standgestaltung
IMM 1998 | IF Hannover, Exhibition
Design Award, Gold, Standgestal-
tung IMM 2001 | Deutscher Designer
Club ,Gute Gestaltung' Grand Prix
2005 – für Lebenswerk Nils Holger
Moormann

Kommunikation
| Auszeichnung Deutscher Designer
Club, DDC 1994, Firmenbroschüre
1994 | Deutscher Preis für Kommuni-
kationsdesign, Design Zentrum Nordrhein-Westfalen, Firmenbroschüre
1996 | Type Directors Club New York,
Award for typografic excellence 1997
Firmenbroschüre 1998 | Deutscher
Preis für Kommunikationsdesign,
Design Zentrum Nordrhein-West-
falen, Firmenbroschüre 1998 | Euro-
pean Design Annual 1999, Firmen-
broschüre 1998 | Good Design
Award 1998, The Chicago Athenæum, Firmenbroschüre 1998
| ,Die schönsten deutschen Bücher
2000', Stiftung Buchkunst, 2000,
Firmenbroschüre 2000 | Shortlist
,Die schönsten deutschen Bücher
2002' Stiftung Buchkunst, 2002,
Firmenbroschüre 2002
| IF Communication Design Award
2004, Firmenbroschüre 2004
| Deutscher Designer Club ,Das gute
Stück', Auszeichnung silber 2005,
Firmenbroschüre 2005 | IF Commu-
nication Design Award 2005 – Auszeichnung in Gold, Präsentation
Messebroschüre auf IMM Cologne
2005

Deutschland
Nils Holger Moormann GmbH
An der Festhalle 2
D-83229 Aschau i. Ch.
Deutschland
T + 49 (0) 80 52-9 04 50
F + 49 (0) 80 52-90 45 45
info@moormann.de
www.moormann.de

Dänemark/Norwegen/Schweden
Christopher Rasmussen
Ørslev Gade 74
DK-4100 Ringsted
Dänemark
T + 45-70 20 23 26
F + 45-70 20 09 50
moormann@crisras.dk
www.crisras.dk

Finnland
Raili Hofmann
Soinistentie 22G33
FI-21100 Naantali
Finnland
T + 358-24 38 30 02
F + 358-24 38 30 02
raili.hofmann@dnainternet.net

Großbritannien
Femke Teunen
25 Montague Avenue
GB-London SE4 1YP
England
T + 44-208-6 91 48 68
F + 44-208-6 91 48 68
mob + 44-79 90 64 76 72
moormann@femke-teunen.com
www.femke-teunen.com

Irland
MiMo Ireland Ltd.
Kilmichael West
Coast Road
IRL-Fountainstown, Co. Cork
Irland
T +353-214 83 34 43
F +353-214 83 34 20
info@mimodesign.ie
www.mimodesign.ie

Niederlande/Belgien
Wonderland
international interior agencies
Jitze P. Baarsma
Weverstraat 12
NL-8861 DX Harlingen
Niederlande
T + 31-5 17 43 05 14
F + 31-5 17 43 05 01
moormann@baarsma-wonderland.nl
www.baarsma-wonderland.nl

Neuseeland
Katalog NZ Ltd.
Furniture and Lighting
PO Box 7511
24 Spring Street
Freemans Bay
NZ-Auckland/New Zealand
Neuseeland
T + 64-93 60 42 90
F + 64-93 60 42 91
greg@katalog.co.nz
www.katalog.co.nz

Impressum

© 2006 Nils Holger Moormann GmbH
Vol. 7
Schutzgebühr EUR 6,–

Erste Auflage
Herausgeber:
Nils Holger Moormann GmbH
Konzept & Gestaltung:
Jäger & Jäger, Kommunikationsdesign
www.jaegerundjaeger.de

Fotonachweis:
Julia Angele: S. 4 | Jäger & Jäger: S. 8, 44,
50, 62, 74, 80, 86, 116, 142, 148, 154, 160, 166,
178 | Jäger & Jäger/iStockphoto: S. 38,
92, 104, 110 | iStockphoto: S. 26, 68, 128, 172
| Josef Reiter: S. 32 | Seite 98 (Dresscode):
Off-Duty Soldiers, © Getty Images/
Douglas Miller | C. Winkler: S. 136
Abb. Möbel:
Lutz Bertram: S. 11, 17, 23, 47, 53, 71, 65, 77,
89, 95, 107, 113, 119, 125, 132, 139, 145, 151, 157,
169, 175 | Tom Vack: S. 131, 132, 133, 163 | Nils
Holger Moormann GmbH: S. 29, 35, 41, 59,
83, 101, 181

Unser Dank gilt Graham Lack für die
englischen Übersetzungen unserer Texte,
sowie Martin Krueger aus Berlin und den
Lakota-Indianern für die Übersetzung
unseres HutAb-Textes in die Sprache der
Lakota. Um die Problematik des wort-
getreuen Übersetzens ein wenig zu ver-
deutlichen, hier eine Rückübersetzung
des Lakota-Textes ins Deutsche:
*„Wann immer Nachtsonne die jene Tages-
sonne die zweimal tötete dann mein Herz
das Flussbiegung die an begraben sollt –
ich gebe Euch eine Anordnung als Mann.
Weißer Heiliger der jener Schlecht-Fühlend-
Seienden medizin-mäßig-helfen kann – ich
stelle dir diese Frage als Mann."*

Papier: Tauro Offset 120 g,
Umschlag: Tauro Offset 300 g

Druck:
bodensee medienzentrum GmbH &
Co. KG, Tettnang

Buchbinderei:
Buchbinderei Haggenmiller GmbH,
Lindenberg/Allgäu

Nils Holger Moormann GmbH
An der Festhalle 2
D-83229 Aschau im Chiemgau
Tel: 0049 (0) 80 52/90 45-0
Fax: 0049 (0) 80 52/90 45-45
www.moormann.de

Verlag Hermann Schmidt Mainz
Robert-Koch-Straße 8
D-55129 Mainz
Tel. 0049 (0) 61 31/50 60 30
Fax 0049 (0) 61 31/50 60 80
info@typografie.de
www.typografie.de

ISBN 3-87439-697-5
ISBN 978-3-87439-697-4
Printed in Germany